Feb 4th 1958

Bonneville Stake High Priests Quorum

Ora H Barlow

Glen F Finlayson

J Elmo Ostler

Somewhere I've Read

✦

A book of meditations to help those
who dare improve themselves; to
those who seek guidance in meeting
their daily problems; and to those
who take what they have and build
their house of happiness . . .

Compiled by

LUCY GERTSCH THOMSON

BOOKCRAFT, INC.

SALT LAKE CITY, UTAH

ACKNOWLEDGMENTS

Sincere appreciation is given to Blodwin Gertsch, the Frodshams, and my husband, James Thomson, for helping type the manuscript. Also to the following for their graciousness in giving consent to publish the following:

To Grace Noll Crowell for her permission to reprint her two poems: "Pain" and "Step by Step," taken from *The Radiant Quest*, by Grace Noll Crowell, Copyright 1948, Harper & Bros.

To Lathrop Lee and Shepherd Company for: "What Killed the Eagle," "The Story of Washington Making Friends," "The Boy With Many Recommendations," "Teaching a Machine to say 'Spezia,'" and "The Match Seller."

To Harper's Magazine for the story, "The Silver Watch."

To abingdon Cokesbury Press for: "Charity," "Seven Deadly Sins," "Reputation vs. Character," taken from the book *Encyclopedia of Wit, Humor and Wisdom*, compiled by Leewin B. Williams.

iii

Dedicated to Jack Carlson and Milo Jacobson, two hospitalized veterans, who are making a magnificent struggle against their adversities.

iv

PREFACE

The purpose of this book is to cause a lifting of the spirits of those who are depressed; to provide a story for a teacher, who may need to illustrate a point or provide a pertinent verse quickly.

Lu Bruyere once said, "When a book raises your spirits and inspires you with noble and manly thoughts, seek no further test of its excellence. It is good and made by a good workman."

The success stories, quotations, and poetry contained in these covers will certainly prove that life can be useful and happy regardless of circumstances.

I sincerely hope that *SOMEWHERE I'VE READ* may bring you hope, and a determination to continue steadfastly on.

Lucy Gertsch Thomson

INDEX

PART I

True Success Stories

PART II

Useful Quotations, Prose, and Poetry

INDEX (cont.)

INDEX (cont.)

Part 1

✦

TRUE
SUCCESS
STORIES

MICHAEL'S TRIUMPH

If you should find yourself giving in to sadness you might consider the life of Michael J. Dowling. When but a young man of fourteen years of age, Michael was overcome by a blizzard in Michigan. Before his parents discovered him, he was frostbitten so badly that he had to undergo amputation of his limbs. His right leg was amputated almost to the hips; his left leg above the knee; his right arm was amputated as well as his left hand.

Can you guess the consequences? He went to the Board of County Commissioners and asked for a loan to educate himself, with a promise that he would pay back every cent he borrowed.

During World War I, Michael Dowling became president of one of the largest banks in St. Paul, but he left his position and went to Europe to help build up the soldiers' morale.

Upon one occasion in London, he lectured to wounded, discouraged soldiers, who were brought to the hotel in the wheel chairs. They were in the lobby, while he was placed on the mezzanine floor. As he began to speak he minimized their wounded condition, and their loss of an eye or arm. He refused to listen to their complaints. His apparently unsympathetic nature angered the wounded men so much that they began to jeer as he continued speaking. Then Michael Dowling began walking down the steps, still reminding them how fortunate they were. They became furious, as he commented further. Finally he sat down and removed his right leg. This surprised them and reduced the anger somewhat, but still they resented his suggestion that they were well off. When he took off his left leg, there was instantaneous silence. Before he had arrived at the bottom of the steps, he had removed his right arm, and left hand. There he sat just a stump of a body.

Did this thwart his usefulness? No, indeed. Besides being bank president, he was the father of five children. He taught the world how to triumph over obstacles, how to make money, and how to rear a family. He finally died from exhaustion as a result of his lectures to World War veterans, encouraging them to face life.

Michael J. Dowling proved something to every person with a handicap: It is not the handicap that causes failure, but the lack of courage to overcome the handicap.

THE ANGEL WITH THE LAMP

Florence Nightingale's colorful life history impels admiration from all who read it.

She was a brilliant, petted child of a prominent and wealthy family in England. Florence was destined for a career as a great society woman. Her parents were intimate with the greatest thinkers of England and France. But Florence was unhappy.

When only sixteen years of age, she broke away from this life of easy society living to lead a life of public service. The occupation of a woman of fashion held absolutely no interest for her. She wanted to be a nurse. To Florence's parents this was unthinkable. Nursing in the nineteenth century was practised by women of the lowest class. All that was expected of the profession in those days was a knowledge of how to make a poultice.

To distract her mind, Florence's parents sent her abroad with friends. Mrs. Nightingale was broken-hearted to think her daughter was interested in nursing. Weeping, she said, "We are ducks, and have hatched a wild swan."

Florence broke away from her family to train in an obscure shack in Germany which was founded as an asylum for discharged female prisoners.

Florence's tenderness in nursing was first noticed when she was a small child. Once she refused to go on a drive with her nurse because she preferred to stay home to take care of her black-eyed cat that someone had injured. She spent hours caring for dolls. She would imagine that they were stricken with a dread disease or fever.

Whenever a cow or dog was in trouble, people sent for Florence. When she was older, she cared for her relatives and poor people in her community.

When stories of the Crimean War came to England, Florence volunteered her services to help the suffering British soldiers. Nearly fifty percent of the British wounded had died because of unsanitary conditions. As a result of Florence's work, she reduced the death rate to less than two in a hundred.

When she went to Scutari, there were insufficient beds, no vessels for water, no clean bedding, soap, hospital clothes, nor furniture. There had been a complete breakdown of medical arrangements by those in authority. Florence didn't blame anyone. She tackled the job.

Her difficulties were numerous. First she had to break down extreme prejudices of both medical and military men. Women nurses in an army hospital were unheard of.

One of the first things she did was to purchase 200 scrubbing brushes. She helped scrub the floors herself. Then she and the other nurses changed all the soldiers' blood-soaked garments to clean ones. Every night she made the hospital rounds, carrying a lamp. As she passed the four miles of beds, she left each soldier a smile and a word of comfort. No wonder the soldiers adored her, and affectionately called her "The Angel of Crimea" and "The Lady with the Lamp."

Once Florence wrote home: "Let no woman come out here who is not used to fatigue and privation." Often she herself was on her feet for twenty-four hours a day.

In addition to her many duties she carried on a huge correspondence. Late in the night, she sat and wrote dying messages for the soldiers, reports to ministers at home, and medical officials.

While visiting at the Balaklava hospitals, Florence contracted the Crimean fever. She lay desperately ill for twelve days and was ordered back to England for a rest. This privilege she refused, saying, "I am ready to stand out the war with any man." She stayed until peace had come, and all the hospitals were closed.

When her work was completed, after the victory bell had tolled, England planned a rousing welcome home. The authorities planned to have three military bands meet her at the station whenever she should arrive. But Florence refused to publish the time of her arrival. She didn't want any spectacular welcome. Quietly she entered through the back door of her old home, unannounced.

Her countrymen, in grateful appreciation for

her nursing efforts, awarded her a fund of $150,-000. This sum Florence spent in establishing the Nightingale Home for Nurses. Training courses were begun throughout the British Isles which served as a pattern for nurses' training.

This "Lady of the Lamp" lived to be ninety years of age. Fifty years of her life were spent in service to humanity.

THE ENCHANTED HILLS

In 1931 Martha Berry was voted one of the greatest women in the United States. The story of her earning this award is one that warms the hearts and fires the imagination.

She had traveled in Europe and returned with longing to the enchanted hills around Mount Berry, Georgia, where her family homestead was situated. She gazed lovingly around the land, and upon entering the house she sat at the organ to play music which recalled memories of this delightful spot where she had spent her young womanhood. As she played, she turned toward the window to catch another view of her beloved hills. Instead, her attention was caught by the sight of scores of undernourished, wide-eyed children peering in at her.

This sight so shocked Martha Berry that she

determined that there should be no more such poverty as was apparent in the looks of these deprived youngsters. Then and there she called them into the room and taught them to sing.

She also taught them Bible stories and other delightful tales.

So delighted were those half-starved, uneducated souls that she said they would repeat the experience the following week.

Hundreds gathered week after week. This hour with the children made her realize that their education would never exceed this learning. She resolved to begin a real school and give each a solid education, as far as her own private means could provide. She was successful, and when her own means expired, she made a trip to Washington to plead the cause of these young people.

Means were granted and today in Mount Berry, Georgia, there stands a good school. There students can pay their own tuition by working part time in the fields and the various workshops attached to the school.

Her system of a self-supporting school gained acceptance near and far. She received many national honors.

The remarkable thing about this famous philanthropist and educator lies in the fact that she could have had a life of travel, ease, and luxury, but rather she chose the larger life — of forgetting self, to think of others. She was born of wealthy, prominent parents and received an excellent education.

She lived to be seventy-six years of age and devoted her entire life to the worthy task of erasing ignorance and want from the lives of hundreds of her fellow beings.

THE UNCONQUERABLE ERNESTINE

When Ernestine Schumann Heink's grandmother predicted that Ernestine would be great, Ernestine's mother said, "What? The child of a poor army officer? How can you tell?"

The grandmother answered, "I don't know, but you'll see."

Schumann-Heink always remembered these encouraging words.

She later was recognized by the world as one of its greatest contralto singers.

Schumann-Heink's life is one of admirable courage. One day during the school noon hour, she wandered into a market, where she found a great circus. She smelled the odor of food and became so very hungry that she knew somehow she must get something to eat. She ventured to ask, saying,

"Please, please give me some food. I will work for it. I'll do anything."

They were surprised and roared with laughter and said, "If you want to work, little one, clean the monkey cage first, then you can eat."

They were just joking, but she wasn't. Quick as a flash, she cleaned the cage. What a meal they gave her!

Thereafter, every day Ernestine went to the circus and the managers let her do things — even promising her she could ride on the horses.

One day an officer of her father's regiment happened to be at the circus and recognized her. When it was reported to her father, he was furious.

"But I was hungry, Father," Ernestine confessed.

In her own words, "Ach, how Father and Mother looked at each other."

After the circus episode, the family was transferred to Hungary and to Prague. Here she was placed in a convent, and it was here that her voice was discovered.

"But, how can we do anything to help her with no fortune, friends, or influence?" asked her mother when it was reported to her about Ernestine's beautiful voice.

"It will surely come! Where God had given

such talent, there will always be a way," suggested Mother Bernardine.

When the good news was told Ernestine's father, he flew into a rage.

"What? What?" he shouted. "A singer — an actress — a bad woman? Never!"

Her mother tried to quiet him by reminding him that not everyone on the stage was bad.

Her father only grumbled, "From where do you get the money?"

Ernestine continued to sing for mass. One day, a former prima donna heard her sing. Immediately she asked Mother Bernardine, "Who was the girl with the contralto voice? In all my long experience I have never heard such a voice."

Mother Bernardine said, "Why, she is a very poor child from an Austrian officer's family."

"Then I must see her immediately."

From this meeting came the first of Ernestine's voice lessons. They continued for a short time only because one day her father announced that they must be transferred to Garz.

All hope was gone, singing lessons were over — what a blow!

Then came a period of more want and hardship. Ernestine's mother gave birth to a child and very nearly died. Ernestine had to manage the household. However, after the mother's recovery, things began to look up. A daughter of an officer in the regiment had formerly been an opera singer. Ernestine's mother talked to the young woman, and after a tryout of Ernestine's voice, the singer, Marietta, enthusiastically gave Ernestine lessons. Her first public singing netted her six dollars. Of this Ernestine gave two dollars to her mother, kept some for herself, then with the rest bought a second-hand cage for her bird. Later she went to Vienna and sang to a director whom she had chanced to meet in Garz.

Her singing was good, but when the directors discussed her, they said, "Go home, quick — buy a sewing machine, or something like that — but never try to be an opera singer! Impossible — short, homely, undernourished, poverty-sticken — no appearance — no, never!"

She returned broken-hearted.

Her father exclaimed, "I told you so — that settles it — you will forget this nonsense, and be a teacher."

Her mother was heartsick, but her teacher, Marietta, was furious. She shouted at Ernestine's father, "Ach! you do not understand — you don't even understand your own child!"

In secret, Ernestine's mother had another conversation with the father. She said, "You are a cruel father. To kill the ambition of your own child is a great sin. I believe she has a gift, and I will prove it to you and the world."

Marietta insisted upon giving Ernestine secret lessons.

Her first opera opportunity came in Dresden, Germany. When she told an old school friend of her opportunity, he handed her 400 gulden and said, "Take them — do anything you want, but for goodness sake get some real clothes, and some shoes," for Ernestine was wearing an old pair of army shoes.

She took his advice, but she saved enough to buy her mother a dress.

While she was singing at the Dresden Opera, Ernestine met Heink, whom she married. Because she married without permission of the superintendent of the opera, she lost her position. Heink was secretary to the Royal Opera, and he lost his position, also, for the same reason. Heink had many debts. Children came until there were four. Then Heink left her. What hunger and struggle followed!

It took twenty years to build Ernestine's career. Her second marriage was to Schumann, an actor. They loved one another deeply, but his illness marred their complete happiness. He died while she was in America, appearing in an opera. To have him die alone nearly broke her heart.

Ernestine had lost her contract in London with the Covent Garden Opera Company because of her great love for her children. She had sung one cycle. The second cycle was beginning. A wire came that her baby was dying in Germany. She didn't even take the paint from her face nor explain anything. Frantically she rushed to her dying baby. She miraculously saved the child's life. Of course, her manager was furious, but later he understood and said, "You can never come back. But I understand."

Schumann's death changed Ernestine's life. She felt incapable of going on alone. Later she married her manager, William Rapp, to whom she turned for protection. She felt incapable of going on with her career and eight children.

The real blow came when she and William Rapp arrived in Germany and learned that because she had married a foreigner, she had forfeited all rights to her money, children, and property. Everything was in Schumann's name.

Ernestine was livid with anger when told she couldn't take her children to the United States.

"My children belong to me," she cried, "and I'll have them." She procured a van and moved furniture and children onto the ship, *Deutschland*. Within forty-eight hours, they were sailing the Atlantic. She knew the minute the children were in the United States they would be protected since she had become an American citizen by her marriage to Rapp.

Of war and death, Ernestine learned a great

deal. She was studying and singing in Germany when the World War broke out. Through her good service in America she was able to be evacuated.

She sang everywhere for the soldiers during the war. Once she had a special engagement. As she was leaving, a soldier lad came and timidly asked if she would sing at a comrade soldier's funeral. Her associates tried to dissuade her, but Schumann-Heink said, "Yes." When she arrived and saw the corpse over whom she was to sing, she wept. It was the son of the man that had taught her to sing "The Star Spangled Banner."

This valiant soul lived to be seventy-five years of age. Throughout these years she experienced almost eevry kind of setback, but her indomitable courage bore her up. Her buoyant spirit, together with her glorious voice, won the hearts of her American compatriots.

THE UNCROWNED KING

The difference between men of great or mediocre lives lies in the difference of their energy and the way they employ their time. This perhaps answers why Thomas Edison excelled above the common lot. Emil Ludwig, the noted biographer, called him the uncrowned king of America. Born in obscurity in Milan, Ohio, Edison rose to be proclaimed the greatest American since Washington and Lincoln. His adventurous career, fighting obstacles of early poverty and many failures, resulted in some 3,000 inventions.

Edison has contributed something to every living American. The glow of the electric light, the theatre on the screen, the telephone transmitter, the phonograph, the voice of the radio, are all wonders he gave to us.

Of his lesser inventions, the medical profession owes thanks for a drug he discovered to overcome gout. The discovery came about when he met an old friend, and observed the swelling of his finger joints.

The friend said, "This is caused by deposits of uric acid in the joints."

"Go to a doctor and let him cure you," suggested Edison.

"They can't, because uric acid is insoluble."

"I don't believe it," said Edison. Immediately he began experimenting. Within forty-eight hours he had found a chemical that dissolved uric acid.

Edison also invented a typewriter, an electric pen, an addressing machine, methods of preserving fruit, the making of plate glass and cast iron. He invented the vote machine and thousands of other useful devices. The war records at Washington officially recognize thirty-nine war inventions by Edison. Some of these devices were underwater searchlights, smudging skylines, mirror reflection for warships.

Edison accomplished his tasks by hours and days of patient effort.

To a man who thought he only worked when the spirit moved him, he said, "Genius is two percent inspiration and 98 percent perspiration." Edison worked for five years on the invention of a new storage battery. He made thousands of experiments. He failed 10,000 times before he perfected the incandescent light. Failure merely spurred him on. Undaunted perseverance was the secret of his success.

At one time an Englishman wrote to Edison stating that he was touring the country with his son. He asked permission to see Edison, since he had a desire that his son should personally meet so great an inventor. Edison was agreeable. Then the Englishman asked Edison to say something to the lad which might influence his life. Edison patted the boy's head and said, "My boy, never watch the clock."

Edison never carried a watch. He would quit when a task was finished. Luther Stieringer once said, "If Edison could have chosen his birthplace, he would have chosen Mars so he could have the advantage of a day forty minutes longer."

What is the main ingredient for success?

In Edison's own words, "Imagination plus ambition and the will to work." Usually Edison was in his laboratory at 7:30 in the morning. His lunch would be sent to him. In the evening he took time out to eat, but he would return at 8 o'clock. His carriage would call for him at 11:30 at night, but often he would keep the coachman waiting for three or more hours. Edison played as he worked. When he went on a vacation, he completely forgot his work.

In his laboratory in Florida, Edison experimented with more than 14,000 different plants in an effort to find their rubber content. Of all the plants he found goldenrod had the highest rubber content. He estimated 100 pounds of rubber to an acre of goldenrod.

Edison was a remarkable personality. He was slightly deaf in one ear, but he regarded it as an asset, saying, "It has saved me from listening to much nonsense which could have resulted in the waste of valuable time." He had an indomitable determination and boundless energy. He was unaffected. It is said the one thing he feared in life was the "bighead."

His kindness was remarkable, and people who knew him best said he seldom became angry or "let himself go." It is said he would often work for two days before sleeping. If for some reason he had to be awakened, and that was accomplished only by severe shaking, he would never show any irritability.

W. S. Mallory, one of his associates, said, "I doubt if there is another man living for whom his men would do so much."

Edison gave credit for most of his inspiration to his mother, who understood him. At one time Edison came home tearfully from school. "The teacher says that I am retarded." Mother Edison's indignation was aroused. Taking him by the hand she brought him back to school and faced the teacher, saying, "You don't know what you are talking about. He has more brains than you have, and that is what is the trouble. I will take him home and teach him myself and show you what can be done with him." She had formerly been a school teacher and she gave him the benefit of her learning.

From his early youth Edison possessed an inquisitiveness which sometimes caused him trouble. His curiosity led him to investigate the secrets of fire. He decided to build a fire in the barn so he could watch its progress. He hadn't expected it to get out of bounds. As a result he barely escaped with his life, and the barn was totally destroyed.

Though the worlds remembers Edison as a man of effort and inventions, his children remember him as an intensely human person. In the words of his son, Thomas, "Father was not so engrossed in his work that he could not spend some time with his children. I remember when he was devising games and recreation for us and the children in the neighborhood. When we came home from school, we waited anxiously for him to arrive; he never failed to bring us some surprise, and usually it was an alarm clock, which he brought by the dozen. It was with keen delight that we took them apart under his supervision."

Edison looked forward. In his eighty-fourth year he said, "I'm through with the past. I'm looking ahead." He still wanted to live fifteen years longer. He said, "It's time enough to retire at one hundred. I'll have to work hard to complete all the things I have in mind by that time." To another who asked when he was going to retire, he said, "The day before the funeral."

Edison's last message was: "Be courageous." The radio broadcast these words from a convention at Atlantic City, "My message to you is to be courageous. I have lived a long time. I have seen history repeat itself again and again. I have seen many depressions in business. Always America has come out strong and more prosperous. Be brave as your fathers were before you. Have faith — go forward."

THAT WONDERFUL MAN

At 4 o'clock one morning in Detroit, Henry gave an exultant cry! It was finished — this car that he had been tinkering with for three years in a woodshed behind his house.

He made it run around the block successfully. Then he made a few adjustments and took his wife and baby for a ride. He drove it often after that, notwithstanding the protests of the angry farmers who had to manage their frightened horses.

All the neighborhood, who had branded him as "Crazy Ford," must have bowed apologetically to this man who organized and later became president of the Ford Motor Company — destined to become one of the world's largest motor manufacturing companies. The neighbors who remembered him as Hank had more than once threatened to remove this nuisance. Experiments with "horseless carriages" made Henry Ford a social outcast.

Ford was born on a farm in Greenfield, Michigan, where he attended grammar school. "But his mind was not on school work nor the farm. Instead he was always found where some wheel turned. He found broken plows, saws, and mended them. He became a master of mechanical skills, though he never learned to spell or read well.

He often got into trouble, because he would persuade his associates to leave school and watch him build water wheels and steam turbines. Constantly he would fix farm implements for his neighbors, always refusing pay. He was an exasperation to his father because he refused to take money for work that he did for others, and because he refused to work on the farm.

His first obsession was gathering old watches and repairing them. Later he built one watch complete from scratch. He had the aim of making a watch for thirty cents. He gave this up because he concluded watches weren't a necessity, and people generally wouldn't buy a luxury. At the age of sixteen he became a machinist's apprentice.

Step by step he advanced until he became an exponent of mass production. One of his greatest achievements was the moving assembly line.

His creation of a car so cheap that almost everyone could own one transformed our American way of life. It necessitated new road construction and promoted new industries.

In 1914 Ford rose to national fame. He made the declaration that he was going to share the profits of his company, which would amount to ten million dollars the first year. He also an-

nounced that he would pay a minimum wage of
five dollars a day — an unheard-of wage at that
time. During that period an unskilled worker was
receiving one dollar a day and a skilled worker
was receiving two dollars and fifty cents a day.

Ford was considered the most powerful man,
economically, on earth. The biggest asset he had
was his brain and the brains of his associates. Had
all Ford's plants been destroyed, the brains which
built the Ford business could have duplicated it
again in a short time.

Someone said that Henry Ford could gather
a billion dollars with no more effort than the
average man would expend in raising the money
with which to pay a month's rent. His secret was
combining determination, persistency, and a well-
defined desire to gather and organize. Man power
is merely organized knowledge expressed through
intelligent effort. Ford had a powerful battle in
overcoming the enemies: illiteracy, ignorance,
and poverty, and he did master them. Anyone
that can master these three savage hindrances
deserves recognition.

As a philanthropist, he did much. He established a trade school for boys. The Edison Insti-
tute School and the Henry Ford Hospital in Detroit are two of the many non-profit enterprises
conducted by him. He also established the Henry
Ford Museum.

Much of his giving he did secretly as is evidenced by the following narrative: One day he visited the farm and found the caretaker scolding a lad, whom he had found sleeping in the hay. "But I couldn't find a place to stay, and I was so tired," replied the lad. "You might have burned down the barn," continued the caretaker.

Henry Ford, who was listening, said, "Come, lad, and I will give you a ride to town." On the way, he discussed the boy's plight. He gave the boy a dollar and an address where he was quite certain he could get employment. When Ford arrived at his office, he called a number and suggested the boy be given a chance.

Weeks later the lad returned to the caretaker on the farm, inquiring, "Could you please tell me the name of the man who gave me that dollar? I'd like to repay him."

"He doesn't wish his name mentioned, but I see him often and will gladly give it to him."

When Ford received the money, he said, "Anyone as appreciative and ambitious as that deserves a break." That boy later became one of Ford's most valuable and highest paid men.

When World War I broke out, Henry tried desperately to bring about peace. When peace efforts failed, he used his plants to capacity in manufacturing war materials.

In World War II his Willow Run plant was

the largest aircraft assembly plant in the world, and made B-24 bombers until the end of the war.

Ford made his marvelous contributions to mankind because he discovered for what he was best fitted, selected his definite chief aim, and then didn't quit until it was accomplished.

Part II

✦

USEFUL
QUOTATIONS,
PROSE,
AND
POETRY

ABILITY

The question "Who ought to be boss?" is like asking "Who ought to be the tenor in the quartet?" Obviously, the man who can sing tenor.—*Henry Ford.*

* * * *

A pint can't hold a quart — if it holds a pint, it is doing all that can be expected of it.—*Margaret Deland.*

ABSENCE

Short absence quickens love; long absence kills it.—*Mirabeau.*

* * * *

Absence in love is like water upon fire; a little quickens but much extinguishes it.—*Hannah Moore.*

ACHIEVEMENT

The greatest of human possessions are a well-trained mind, a body to match, and a love of achievement, without which a man is old before his time.—*Unknown.*

* * * *

Do your work well — God's recompense to you is the power to do greater things.—*Anon.*

* * * *

A man is no greater than his thoughts, decisions, and faith.—*Anon.*

* * * *

What we have done for ourselves alone dies with us. What we have done for others and the world remains and is immortal.—*Albert Pipe.*

* * * *

We are all blind until we see that in the human plan nothing is worth the making if it does not make the man.—*Anon.*

* * * *

The worst wheel of the cart makes the most noise.—*Anon.*

* * * *

The real difference between men is energy. A strong will, a settled purpose, an invincible determination can accomplish almost anything, and in this lies the destination between great men and little men.—*Anon.*

Great minds have great purpose, others have only wishes.—*Washington Irving.*

* * * *

The object of teaching a child is to enable him to get along without his teacher.—*Elbert Hubbard.*

* * * *

The most disastrous times have produced the greatest minds. The purest metal comes of the most ardent furnace; the most brilliant lightning comes of the darkest clouds.—*Chateaubriand.*

* * * *

Great souls suffer in silence.—*Schiller.*

* * * *

There are three kinds of people: those who make things happen; those who watch things happen; and those who have no idea what has happened.—*Anon.*

ACQUAINTANCE

If a man does not make new acquaintances as he advances through life, he will soon find himself left alone; one should keep his friendships in constant repair.—*Johnson.*

* * * *

Never say you know a man till you have divided an inheritance with him.—*Lavater.*

ADVERSITY

Prosperity is no just scale; adversity is the only balance to weigh friends.—*Plutarch.*

* * *

Who hath not known ill fortune, never knew himself, or his own virtues.—*Mallet.*

* * * *

Prosperity is a great teacher; adversity is a greater. Possession pampers the mind; privation trains and strengthens it.—*Hazlitt.*

* * *

He that has no cross will have no crown.—*Quarles.*

* * * *

A smooth sea never made a skillful mariner, neither do uninterrupted prosperity and success qualify for usefulness and happiness. The storms of adversity, like those of the ocean, rouse the faculties and excite the invention, prudence, skill, and fortitude of the voyager. The martyrs of ancient times, in bracing their minds to outward calamities, acquired a loftiness of purpose and a moral heroism worth a lifetime of softness and security.—*Anon.*

AGE

We do not count a man's years until he has nothing else to count.—*Emerson.*

* * * *

Men of age object too much, consult too long, adventure too little, repent too soon, and seldom drive business home to the full period but content themselves with mediocrity of success.—*Bacon.*

* * * *

Forty is the old age of youth, fifty is the youth of old age.—*Victor Hugo.*

ANGER

When Stuart was painting Washington's portrait, he was rallied one day by the general for his slow work. The painter protested that his picture could not advance until the canvas was dry and that there must be yet some delay. Upon arriving the next morning Stuart turned to his canvas and discovered, to his great sorrow, that his picture was spoiled. "General," said he, "someone has held this picture to the fire." Washington summoned his Negro valet, Sam, and demanded in great indignation who had dared to touch the portrait. The trembling Sam replied that, chancing to overhear Washington's expression of impatience at the slowness of the work, and the response of the artist that it must be dry before he could go on, he had ventured to put the canvas before the fire. Washington in great anger dismissed him and told him not to show his face again. But the next day, after Stuart had arrived and was preparing to work, Washington rang the bell and sent for Sam. He came in abashed and trembling. The President drew a new silver watch from his pocket and said, "Come here, Sam. Take this watch and, whenever you look at it, remember that your master, in a moment of passion said to you what he now regrets and that he was not ashamed to confess that he had done so."—*Harper's Magazine*, Dec. 1854. (Used by permission.)

* * * *

Just "keeping still" is one of the finest things a young person can acquire. It doesn't matter so much what someone says. It is what you say in reply, nine times out of ten, that makes the quarrel.

* * * *

The strong character can be quiet under abuse or misrepresentation, and the storm will leave it stronger than it was before.

* * * *

Making an issue of little things is one of the surest ways to spoil happiness.

To be angry about trifles is mean and childish; to rage and be furious is brutish; and to maintain perpetual wrath is akin to the practice and temper of devils; but to prevent and suppress rising resentment is wise and glorious, is manly and divine.—*Watts.*

* * * *

The greatest remedy for anger is delay. — *Seneca.*

* * * *

All anger is not sinful, because some degree of it, and on some occasions, is inevitable. But it becomes sinful and contradicts the rule of scripture when it is conceived upon slight and inadequate provocation, and when it continues long.—*Paley.*

ASSOCIATES

Tell me with whom thou art found, and I will tell thee who thou art.—*Goethe.*

* * * *

Be very circumspect in the choice of thy company. In the society of thine equals thou shalt enjoy more pleasure; in the society of thy superiors thou shalt find more profit. To be the best in the company is the way to grow worse; the best means to grow better is to be the worst there.— *Quarles.*

It is only when men associate with the wicked with the desire and purpose of doing them good, that they can rely upon the protection of God to preserve them from contamination.—*C. Hodge.*

BELIEF

Remember that what you believe will depend very much on what you are.—*Anon.*

BOASTING

Where there is much pretention, much has been borrowed; nature never pretends.—*Lavater.*

* * * *

Men of real merit, whose noble and glorious deeds we are ready to acknowledge, are not yet to be endured when they vaunt their own actions.—*Aeschines.*

* * * *

Lord Bacon told Sir Edward Coke when he was boasting, "The less you speak of your greatness, the more shall I think of it."

CENSURE

The readiest and surest way to get rid of censure is to correct ourselves.—*Demosthenes.*

Few persons have sufficient wisdom to prefer censure, which is useful, to praise which deceives them.—*La Rochefoucauld*.

CHARACTER

A good character is, in all cases, the fruit of personal exertion. It is not inherited from parents; it is not created by external advantages; it is no necessary appendage of birth, wealth, talents, or station; but it is the result of one's own endeavors — the fruit and reward of good principles manifested in a course of virtuous and honorable action.—*J Hawes*.

* * * *

Character is the result of two things: mental attitude and the way we spend our time.—*Elbert Hubbard*.

* * * *

Never does a man portray his own character more vividly than in his manner of portraying another.—*Richter*.

* * * *

You can tell the character of every man when you see how he receives praise.—*Seneca*.

CHARITY

Every good act is charity. Your smiling in your brother's face is charity; an exhortation of your fellow man to virtuous deeds is equal to almsgiving; your putting a wanderer in the right road is charity; your assisting the blind is charity; your removing stones and thorns and other obstructions from the road is charity; your giving water to the thirsty is charity. A man's true wealth hereafter is the good he does in this world to his fellow man. When he dies, people will say, "What property has he left behind him?" But the angels will ask, "What good deeds has he sent before him?"—*Mahomet.*

* * * *

The charity that hastens to proclaim its good deeds ceases to be charity and is only pride and ostentation.—*Hutton.*

* * * *

He who has never denied himself for the sake of giving has but glanced at the joys of charity.
—*Swetchine.*

CHILDREN

I love little children — and it is not a slight thing when they, who are fresh from God, love us.—*Dickens.*

Are you guilty of constantly criticizing your children? Two young boys were closely examining a work of art on exhibit. Suddenly they heard footsteps, and one exclaimed to the other, "Let's go! They'll think we did it."

* * * *

No parent should spend all his time in the garden of a child's life digging up weeds; there is always danger of scratching out flowers not yet above the ground.

* * * *

Aristippus, being asked what were the most necessary things for well-born boys to learn, replied, "Those things which they will put into practice when they become men."

* * * *

The object of teaching a child is to enable him to get along without his teacher.—*Elbert Hubbard.*

* * * *

A LITTLE CHILD SHALL LEAD THEM

You, little child, with your shining eyes and dimpled cheeks, you can lead us along the pathway to the more abundant life.

We blundering grownups need in our lives the virtues that you have in yours:

The *joy and enthusiasm* of looking forward to each new day with glorious expectations of wonderful things to come;

The *vision* that sees the world as a splendid place with good fairies, brave knights, and glistening castles reaching towards the sky;

The *radiant curiosity* that finds adventure in simple things: the mystery of billowy clouds, the miracle of snowflakes, the magic of growing flowers;

The *tolerance* that forgets the difference as quickly as your childish quarrels are spent; that holds no grudges, that hates never, that loves people for what they are;

The *genuineness of being oneself;* to be done with sham, pretense, and empty show; to be simple, natural, and sincere.

The *courage* that rises from defeat and tries again, as you with laughing face rebuild the house of blocks that topples to the floor;

The *believing heart* that trusts others, knows no fear, and has faith in a Divine Father who watches over his children from the sky;

The *contented, trusting mind* that, at the close of day woos the blessings of childlike slumber;

Little child, we would become like you, that we may find again the kingdom of heaven within our hearts.—*Anon.*

CONDUCT

Washington's rules of conduct:

It is better to be alone than in bad company.
... Undertake not what you cannot perform, but
be careful to keep your promise. ... Speak not
evil of the absent, for it is unjust. ... Labor to
keep alive in your breast that little spark of celes-
tial fire called conscience.

CONSCIENCE

Conscience warns us as a friend before it
punishes as a judge.—*Stanislaus.*

* * * *

Trust that man in nothing who has not a conscience in everything.—*Laurence Sterne.*

COURAGE

Are you having difficulty? Have you lost hope?
Take courage from a man who overcame all these
feelings, and succeeded.

Death took the life of his mother when he was
just nine years of age. When Abraham Lincoln

was but a young man, he ran for the legislature in Illinois but was badly defeated.

He entered business with a partner who proved to be worthless. After the business failed, he spent seventeen years of his life working to pay the debts that his dishonest partner had left him.

He became engaged to Ann Rutledge, a beautiful girl, from New Salem, his first and only true love, and she died. He proposed to Mary Owens a year or two later and was rejected.

After a courtship and one broken engagement with another, Mary Todd, he finally married but was never completely happy in his marriage.

Of Lincoln's four children, all died but one when they were young.

He ran for Congress and was badly defeated. He tried to get an appointment in the United States land office but was unsuccessful.

He was badly defeated when he became a candidate for the United States Senaet.

In 1858 he was defeated by Stephen A. Douglas. His associate, Stanton, publicly ridiculed him, as well as many others, whom he regarded as friends.

Through all these loses and disappointments, Abraham Lincoln remained cheerful and carried on with a quiet determination. He later became the President of the United States and is today respected among all peoples.

The best point from which to attack any problem is the Try-angle.—*Anon.*

* * * *

Christ changes all our sunsets into dawn.—*Clement of Alexandria.*

* * * *

God grant me the serenity to accept the things I cannot change; the courage to change the things I can; and the wisdom to know the difference.—*Dr. Reinhold Niebuhr.*

* * * *

The more the statue grows.—*Anon.*
The more the marble wastes

* * * *

He who loses wealth loses much;
He who loses a friend loses more;
But he that loses his courage loses all.
—*Cervantes.*

* * * *

Too much sun makes a desert.—*Arab Maxim.*

* * * *

He who sacrifices most will be remembered longest in the hearts of his fellow men.

* * * *

THE UNCONQUERABLE MIND

If you think you'll lose, you've lost,
For out in the world you'll find
Success begins with a person's will—
It's all in the state of mind.

Life's battles don't always go
To the stronger or faster man,
But sooner or later the man who wins
Is the fellow who thinks he can.—*Anon.*

* * * *

The most sublime courage I have ever witnessed has been among that class too poor to know they possessed it and too humble for the world to discover it.—*George Bernard Shaw.*

* * * *

The tree that never had to fight
For sun and sky and air and light,
That stood out in the open plain,
And always got its share of rain,
Never became a forest king.

The man who never had to toil,
Who never had to win his share
Of sun and sky and light and air,
Never became a manly man,
But lived and died as he began.

Good timber does not grow in ease;
The stronger wind, the tougher trees;
The more the storm, the more the strength;
By sun and cold, by rain and snow,
In tree or man, good timber grows.

Where thickest stands the forest growth,
We find the patriarchs of both,

And they hold converse with the stars,
Whose broken branches show the scars
Of many winds and much of strife.
This is the common law of life.

> —*Author Unknown.*

COURTESY

He who reflects on another man's want of
breeding, shows he wants it as much himself.—
Plutarch.

* * * *

A broom salesman, seeing an advertisement of
an apartment for sale, opened the door and
walked in. When the manager saw the man, his
brooms over his shoulder, he shouted angrily,
"We want no brooms today," and motioned him
out the door.

The following week, the broom salesman saw
the picture of this same apartment advertised by
another real estate firm. When he went in, he
was received graciously. Before the broom salesman left, he made out a check for enough to buy
the apartment.

The lesson would seem obvious: Courtesy is
due all — regardless of appearances — as the
first real estate man learned to his sorrow.

IF YOU ARE WELL BRED . . .

You will be kind.

You will not use slang.

You will try to make others happy.

You will never indulge in ill-natured gossip.

You will never forget the respect due to age.

You will not answer or boast of your achievements.

You will think of others before you think of yourself.

You will not measure your activity by people's bank accounts.

You will be scrupulous in your regard for the rights of others.

You will not forget engagements, promises, obligations of any kind.

You will never make fun of the peculiarities of others.

You will never, in any circumstances, cause pain to another if you can help it.

You will not think good intentions compensate for rude or gruff manners.

You will be agreeable to your social inferiors as to your equals and superiors.

You will not have two sets of manners — one for company and one for home use.

You will never remind a cripple of his deformity or probe the sore spot of a sensitive soul.

You will not attract attention by either your loud talk or laughter or show your egotism by trying to monopolize conversation.

* * * *

Fine manners need the support of fine manners in others.—*Emerson.*

* * * *

True politeness is perfect ease and freedom. It simply consists in treating others just as you love to be treated yourself.—*Chesterfield.*

* * * *

THE BOY WITH MANY RECOMMENDATIONS

When a merchant had hired an office boy out of fifty applicants who answered his advertisement, a friend asked:

"How did you come to select that fellow? He didn't have a single recommendation."

"He had a great many," replied the merchant. "He wiped his feet when he came in; and he closed the door after him, showing that he is careful. He gave up his seat to a lame old man, showing that he is kind and thoughtful. He took off his cap when he came in and answered my questions promptly and respectfully, showing that he is polite and gentlemanly. He picked up a book which I had purposely laid on the floor and replaced it on the table, while all the rest of the boys stepped over it or shoved it aside. And he waited his turn quietly, instead of pushing or crowding. When I talked to him, I noticed that his clothes were carefully brushed, his hair in nice order, and his teeth as white as milk; and when he wrote his name, I noticed that his fingernails were clean, instead of being tipped with jet like those of that handsome little fellow in the blue jacket. Don't you call all these things letters of recommendation? I do; and I would give more for what I can tell about a boy by using my eyes ten minutes than for all the letters of recommendation he can give me."

A mother in teaching her boy good manners and habits of self-respect may be providing him with a capital more substantial than a bank account.

I have known a good many boys and some men who make fun of those who take care to dress tidily and attractively. Yet young people who have a little pride in making themselves presentable, and whose faces are often wreathed in loving, happy smiles, are most likely to make friends.

Not long ago a prominent business firm discharged their manager because he was never tidy in his personal appearance. When they advertised, they receivd forty applications for the place; yet only one young man was asked to call again.

"Did you observe his neatly fitting shirt and necktie?" asked one of the partners after he had gone, "how nicely his boots were polished, and how tidy he was?"

The young man's references were looked up, and he was engaged the next morning. Several of the others might have been better men for the position, but a first impression is lasting.

In this land of opportunity the cases are very rare where the poorest boy or man ever needs to appear to poor advantage. A man's clothes may be threadbare and even patched; but if they are well brushed and if he is clean himself, his shoes polished, his hair well brushed, and his nails clean, he will command the respect of everyone.

DEATH

When all our hopes are gone,
'Tis well our hands must still keep toiling on,
For others' sake;
For strength to bear is found in duty done,
And he is blessed indeed who learns to make
The joy of others cure his own heartache.—*Anon.*

* * * *

Who ne'er his bread in sorrow ate,
Who ne'er the mournful midnight hours
Weeping upon his bed has sate,
He knows you not, ye heavenly powers.

—*Longfellow.*

Death is one of those inexplicable items of life that robs, and in the robbing gives something in return.

FAILURE

He only is exempt from failures who makes no efforts—*Whatley.*

* * * *

There is only one real failure in life that is possible, and that is, not to be true to the best one knows.—*Farrar.*

* * * *

A certain minister spent considerable time preparing his Sunday sermon. When the time arrived for him to deliver it, there was but one lone visitor in his audience. He debated whether or not to waste his sermon on just one soul. However, his obligation as a minister caused him to discuss the matter with his visitor. In reply, the visitor said:

"Well, I don't know much. I am just an old cow hand. But I know that if I had a load of hay and I only had one cow that was hungry, I believe I'd feed her."

This convinced the minister, and he proceeded to give his sermon. After about an hour he looked at his visitor and discovered he had fallen fast asleep. He preached louder, but his subject remained fast asleep. Finally, he walked to the bench and woke him.

"I don't think I should continue, when you can't follow me," suggested the minister.

"Well, I don't know much," the cow hand admitted, "but, brother, I know this: If I had a load of hay, and one hungry cow, I'd feed her, but I don't think I'd give her the whole load."

* * * *

Christianity hasn't failed — it hasn't been tried.

* * * *

A scarcity of worms doesn't make a hen quit scratching.

FEAR

The people to fear are not those who disagree with you, but those who disagree with you and are too cowardly to let you know.—*Napoleon.*

* * * *

He who has conquered doubt and fear, has conquered failure.—*Anon.*

* * * *

I have generally found that the man who is good at excuses is good for nothing else.

It was good counsel that Jones heard given to

a young person: "Always do what you are afraid to do."—*Emerson.*

* * * *

A railroad shopman had been drawn on a federal grand jury, and did not want to serve. When his name was called, he asked the judge to excuse him. "We are very busy at the shops," he said, "and I ought to be there."

"So you are one of those men who think the railroad could not get along without you," remarked the judge.

"No, your honor," said the shopman, "I know they could get along without me, but I don't want them to find it out."

"Excused," said the judge.

FORGETTING

If you were busy being kind,
Before you knew it you would find
You'd soon forget to think 'twas true
That someone was unkind to you.

If you were busy being glad
And cheering people who seem sad,
Although your heart might ache a bit,
You'd soon forget to notice it.

If you were busy being good,
And doing just the best you could,
You'd not have time to blame some man
Who's doing just the best he can.

> If you were busy being true
> To what you know you ought to do,
> You'd be so busy you'd forget
> The blunders of the folks you've met.

If you were busy being right,
You'd find yourself too busy quite
To criticize your brother long,
Because he's busy being wrong.

FORGIVENESS

He that cannot forgive others breaks the bridge over which he must pass himself, for every man has need to be forgiven.—*Herbert*.

FRIENDSHIP

If a man does not make new acquaintances as he passes through life, he will soon find himself left alone. A man should keep his friendships in constant repair.—*Johnson*.

We take care of our health; we lay up money; we make our roof tight and our clothing sufficient, but who provides wisely that he shall not be wanting in the best property of all — friends?—*Emerson*.

* * * *

MAKING FRIENDS

If nobody smiled and nobody cheered and nobody helped us along;

If every man looked after himself and good things all went to the strong;

If nobody cared just a little for you, and nobody thought about me

And we all stood alone in the battle of life, what a dreary old world this would be!

Life is sweet because of the friends we've made. All things in common we share.

We want to live on, not because of ourselves, but because of the people who care.

It's giving and doing for somebody else — on that all life's splendor depends;

And the joy of the world when you sum it all up, is formed in the making of friends.—*Anon*.

DESTROYING ENEMIES THE
FRIENDLY WAY

President Lincoln was once criticized for his attitude toward his enemies.

"Why do you try to make friends of them?" asked an associate. "You should try to destroy them."

"Am I not destroying my enemies," Lincoln gently replied, "when I make them my friends?"

* * * *

Don't lend money to your friends — you will lost them both.—*Anon.*

* * * *

What wealth it is to have friends that we cannot think of without elevation.—*Thoreau.*

* * * *

Unless you make allowances for your friends' foibles, you betray your own.—*Syrus.*

* * * *

When befriended, remember it;
When you befriend, forget it.—*Franklin.*

* * * *

Nothing can be more disgraceful than to be at war with him with whom you have lived on terms of friendship.—*Cicero.*

* * * *

"What is the secret of your life?" asked Mrs.

Browning of Charles Kingsley. "Tell me that I
may make mine beautiful, too."

He replied, "I have a friend."—*William Chan-
ning.*

* * * *

A STORY OF WASHINGTON
MAKING FRIENDS

An interesting story is told of the first President of the United States, who learned early in
life to control his temper.

Washington, in his very early manhood, had a
heated discussion with a Mr. Payne, in which he
uttered something very offensive. Payne immediately knocked the young officer down. Washington next day sent for him; Payne expected a
challenge or something like that. But Washington
came up to him: "Mr. Payne," he said, "to err is
natural; to rectify error is glory. I believe I was
wrong yesterday; you have already had some satisfaction, and, if you deem that sufficient, here is
my hand; let us be friends." Payne accepted the
hand of reconciliation.

Many years after when Washington had become the first man in America, Payne, passing by,
stopped at Mount Vernon, though feeling somewhat anxious as to his reception. Washington received him cordially, and introduced him to Mrs.

Washington with some playful reminder of the past.

It is, indeed, the glory of a man to rectify his own error. One may be sensitive and easily provoked; yet he is a heroic man, and governed by a divine impulse, if he restrains his indignation and forgives injuries.

* * * *

I have heard a rule that was observed by a Quaker, with excellent results. When he was asked by a merchant whom he had conquered by his patience how he had been able to bear the abuse given him, he replied: "Friend, I will tell thee. I was naturally as hot and violent as thou art. Yet, when I observed that men in a passion always speak loud, I thought if I could control my voice, I should repress my passion. I have therefore made it a rule never to let my voice rise above a certain key; and by careful observance of this rule I have, by the blessing of God, entirely mastered my tongue."

We hear people complain that they cannot restrain their temper. If so, it is because they did not begin soon enough. The time to begin is in early youth.

FREEDOM

There are two freedoms — the false where a man is free to do what he likes; the true, where a man is free to do what he ought.—*Kingsley.*

* * * *

A pessimist is a person who, when given a choice between two evils, choses both of them.—*Anon.*

GOODNESS

Don't be just good, be good for something.—*Anon.*

* * * *

From the same flower the serpent draws poison, and the bee honey.

* * * *

Each time I pass a church
I always pay a visit,
So when at last I'm carried in,
The Lord won't say, "Who is it?"

* * * *

Die when I may, I want it said of me by those who knew me best, that I always plucked a thistle and planted a flower where I thought a flower would grow.—*Abraham Lincoln.*

When we cannot find contentment in ourselves, it is useless to seek it elsewhere.—*La Rochefoucauld*.

* * * *

The weakest among us has a gift, however seemingly trivial, which is peculiar to him, and which worthily used will be a gift also to his race. —*Ruskin*.

* * * *

Life must be measured by thought and action, not by time.—*Lubbock*.

* * * *

Taking the first step with a good thought, the second with a good word, and the third with a good deed, I entered paradise.—*Zoroaster*.

* * * *

It isn't necessary to blow out the other person's light in order to let your own light shine.— *Anon*.

* * * *

There is no limit to the good a man can do, if he doesn't care who gets the credit.—*Anon*.

* * * *

The smallest good deed is better than the grandest intention.—*Anon*.

* * * *

You are a real Saint if you feel just a little ashamed of your very fine clothes when you see your neighbor in rags.

I KNOW SOMETHING GOOD
ABOUT YOU

Wouldn't this old world be better
If the folks we meet would say,
"I know something good about you"
And then treat us just that way?

Wouldn't it be fine and dandy
If each handclasp warm and true
Carried with it this assurance,
"I know something good about you!"

Wouldn't life be lots more happy
If the good that's in us all
Were the only thing about us
That folks bothered to recall?

Wouldn't life be lots more happy
If we praised the good we see,
For there's such a lot of goodness
In the worst of you and me.

Wouldn't it be nice to practice
That fine way of thinking, too?
You know something good about me?
I know something good about you!

* * * *

Somebody did a golden deed;
Somebody proved a friend in need;

Somebody sang a beautiful song;
Somebody smiled the whole day long;
Somebody thought, " 'Tis sweet to live";
Somebody said, "I'm glad to give";
Somebody fought a valiant fight;
Somebody lived to shield the right;
Was that "Somebody" you?

HABIT

First you take the train, then the train takes
you. First the stream makes the bed, then the bed
guides the stream.—*Anon.*

* * * * *

"Habit" is hard to overcome;
　　If you take off the first letter,

It doesn't change a bit.
　　If you take off another,

You have a "bit" left.
　　If you take still another,

The whole of "it" remains.
　　If you take still another,

It is not "t-totally" used up.
　　All of which goes to show

That if you wish to be rid of a "habit"
You have to throw it off together.

HAPPINESS

Happiness in this world, when it comes, comes incidentally. Make it the object of pursuit, and it leads us a wild-goose chase and is never attained.—*Hawthorne.*

* * * *

The belief that youth is the happiest time of life is founded on a fallacy. The happiest person is the person who thinks the most interesting thoughts, and we grow happier as we grow older.—*William Lyon Phelps.*

* * * *

The happiest women, like the happiest nations, have no history.—*George Eliot.*

* * * *

No thoroughly occupied man was ever very miserable.—*L. E. Landon.*

* * * *

True happiness consists not in the multitude of friends, but in their worth and choice.—*Ben Johnson.*

* * * *

Happiness consists in activty; such as the constitution of our nature; it is a running stream, and not a stagnant pool.—*Anon.*

* * * *

No one can secure happiness without earning it.—*Anon.*

A SHORT, SHORT, SHORT STORY

One day a young man found a $5.00 bill between the ties of a railroad. From that time on he never lifted his eyes from the ground while walking. In thirty years, he accumulated 25,916 buttons, 62,172 pins, 7 pennies, a bent back, and a sour, miserly disposition. In "finding" all this, he lost the smiles of his friends, the songs of the birds, the beauties of nature, and the opportunity to serve his fellow man and spread happiness.— *Author Unknown.*

* * * *

THE ROAD TO HAPPINESS

Keep skid-chains on your tongue; always say less than you think. Cultivate a low, persuasive voice. How you say it often counts far more than "what you say."

Make promises sparingly and keep them faithfully, no matter what it costs you.

Never let an opportunity pass to say a kind and encouraging thing to or about somebody. Praise good work done, regardless of who did it. If criticism is merited, criticize helpfully and never spitefully.

Be interested in others: interested in their pursuits, their welfare, their homes, and families. Make merry with those who rejoice and mourn with those who weep. Let everyone you meet, however humble, feel that you regard him as a person of importance.

Be cheerful. Keep the corners of your mouth turned up. Hide your pains, worries, and disappointments under a pleasant smile. Laugh at good stories and learn to tell them.

Preserve an open mind on all debatable questions. Discuss, but don't argue. It is the mark of superior minds to disagree and yet be friendly.

Let your virtues, if you have any, speak for themselves, and refuse to talk of another's vices. Discourage gossip. Make it a point to say nothing to another unless it is something good.

Be careful of others' feelings. Wit at the other fellow's expense is rarely worth the effort and may hurt where least expected.

Pay no attention to ill-natured remarks about you. Simply live so that nobody will believe them. Disordered nerves and bad digestion are common causes of backbiting.

Don't be too anxious about getting your just dues. Do your work, be patient, keep your disposition sweet, forget self, and you will be respected and rewarded.

* * * *

The price of peace is righteousness.

When people yearn with all their hearts
For just one treasure far away,
They close their eyes to countless joys
That crowd around them everyday.—*Anon.*

*   *   *   *

If I had but two loaves of bread, I would sell
one and buy hyacinths, for they would feed my
soul.—*The Koran.*

*   *   *   *

Happiness is the art of never holding in your
mind the memory of any unpleasant thing that
has passed.—*Anon.*

*   *   *   *

He alone is the happy man who has learned
to extract happiness, not from ideal conditions but
from actual ones about him.

*   *   *   *

RULES FOR A PERFECT DAY

Here are ten resolutions to make when you
wake in the morning:

1. Just for today, I will try to live through this
day only and not tackle my whole life problem
at once. I can do some things for twelve hours
that would appal me if I felt I had to keep them
up for a lifetime.

2. Just for today, I will be happy. This as-
sumes that what Abraham Lincoln said is true
that "most folks are about as happy as they make

up their minds to be." Happiness is from within—
it is not a matter of externals.

3. Just for today, I will adjust myself to what
is and not try to adjust everything to my own
desires. I will take my family, my business, and
my luck as they come and fit myself to them.

4. Just for today, I will take care of my body.
I will exercise it, care for it, and nourish it and
not abuse it nor neglect it, so that it will be a perfect machine for my will.

5. Just for today, I will try to strengthen my
mind. I will study. I will learn something useful.
I will not be a mental loafer all day. I will read
something that requires effort, thought, and con-
centration.

Just for today, I will exercise my soul in three
ways. I will do somebody a good turn and not get
found out; if anybody knows it, it will not count.
I will do at least two things I don't want to do, as
William James suggests, just for exercise. I will
not show anyone that my feelings are hurt. They
may be hurt, but today I will not show it.

7. Just for today, I will be agreeable. I will
look as well as I can, dress as becomingly as possible, talk low, act courteously, be liberal with flat-
tery, criticize not one bit nor find fault with anything, and not try to regulate nor improve anyone.

8. Just for today, I will have a program. I
will write down just what I expect to do every

hour. I may not follow it exactly, but I'll have it. It will save me from the two pests — hurry and indecision.

9. Just for today, I will have a quiet half hour, all by myself, and relax. In this half hour, some time, I will think of God, in order to get a little more perspective to my life.

10. Just for today, I will be unafraid, especially I will not be afraid to be happy, to enjoy what is beautiful, to love and to believe that those I love, love me.—*Anon.*

HEALTH

Joy, temperance, and repose, slam the door on the doctor's nose.—*Longfellow.*

* * * *

Bad men live that they may eat and drink, whereas good men eat and drink that they may live.—*Socrates.*

* * * *

We squander health
In search of wealth;
We scheme and toil, and save,
Then squander wealth
In search of health;
And all we get's the grave;

We live and boast
Of what we own;
We die and only get a stone.—*Anon.*

* * * *

Nature does not exact payment for broken laws at the time of breaking — but sometimes thirty years after.

HELPING

You cannot help men permanently by doing for them what they could and should do for themselves.—*Lincoln.*

* * * *

Try to be nice to everyone until you have made your first million; after that they'll be nice to you.—*Anon.*

HONESTY

THE MATCH-SELLER

"Please, sir, buy some matches!" said a little boy, with a poor, thin, blue face, his feet bare and red, and his clothes only a bundle of rags, although it was very cold in Edinburgh that day.

"No, I don't want any," said the gentleman.

"But they're only a penny a box," the little fellow pleaded.

"Yet, but you see I don't want a box."

"Then I'll gie ye two boxes for a penny," the boy said at last.

"And so to get rid of him," said the gentleman who tells the story, "I bought a box; but then I found I had no change, so I said, 'I'll buy a box tomorrow.'"

"Oh, do buy them tonight!" the boy pleaded again; "I'll run and get you the change, for I'm very hungry."

So I gave him the shilling, and he started away. I waited for the boy, but no boy came. Then I thought I had lost my shilling; but still there was that in the boy's face I trusted, and I did not like to think badly of him.

Late in the evening a servant came and said a little boy wanted to see me. When the child was brought in, I found it was a smaller brother of the boy who got the shilling, but, if possible, still more ragged and thin and poor. He stood a moment diving into his rags, as if he were seeking something, and then said, "Are you the gentleman that bought the matches from Sandie?"

"Yes."

"Well, then here's fourpence out of your shilling. Sandie cannot come. He's not well. A cart ran over him and knocked him down, and he lost his cap, and his matches, and your elevenpence; and both his legs are broken, and he's not well at all, and the doctor says he'll die. And that's all he can give you now," putting fourpence down on the table. And then the child broke down in great sobs. So I fed the little man, and then I went with him to see Sandie.

I found that the two little things lived with a wretched, drunken stepmother; their own father and mother were both dead. I found poor Sandie lying on a bundle of shavings. He knew me as soon as I came in, and said: "I got the change, sir, and was coming back; and then the horse knocked me down, and both my legs are broken."

"And Reuby, little Reuby! I am sure I am dying! And who will take care of you, Reuby, when I am gone? What will you do, Reuby?"

Then I took the poor little sufferer's hand, and told him I would always take care of Reuby. He understood me, and had just strength to look at me as if he would thank me. Then the expression went out of his blue eyes; and in a moment —

"He lay within the light of God,
    Like a babe upon the breast,
Where the wicked cease from troubling,
    And the weary are at rest."

What was life to that little match-boy but honesty, truth, nobility, sincerity, genuineness — the qualities that make the highest manhood?

HOPE

If you think you cannot do very much and that the little you can do is of no value, think on these things:

A teakettle singing on a stove was the beginning of the steam engine.

A shirt waving on the clothesline was the beginning of a balloon, the forerunner of the Graf Zeppelin.

A spider web strung across a garden path suggested the suspension bridge.

A lantern swinging in a tower was the beginning of a pendulum.

An apple falling from a tree was the cause of discovering the law of gravitation.

HUMAN RELATIONS

Ten commandments of human relations:

1. Speak to people. There is nothing as nice as a cheerful word of greeting.

2. Smile at people. It takes 72 muscles to frown, only 13 to smile.

3. Call people by name. The sweetest music to anyone's ears is the sound of his own name.

4. Be friendly and helpful. If you would have friends, be friendly.

5. Be cordial. Speak and act as sf everything you do is a genuine pleasure.

6. Be genuinely interested in people. You can like everybody if you try.

7. Be generous with praise — cautious with criticism.

8. Be considerate with the feelings of others. It will be appreciated.

9. Be thoughtful of the opinions of others. There are three sides to a controversy — yours — the other fellow's — and the right one.

10. Be alert to give service. What counts most in life is what we do for others.

* * * *

Quarrels would not last long if the fault were only on one side.—*La Rochefoucauld.*

* * * *

There are many things about human nature which none of us will ever understand. However, as we grow older and gain experience, we formulate for ourselves certain rules which make life easier for ourselves and more pleasant for those who share the world with us.

A wise man experienced in the ways of human nature reached a number of interesting conclusions which are worth preserving for the study of all mankind. They are simple and direct and give considerable food for thought. These were an endowment to me, and I would like to share them:

1. Sooner or later, a man, if he is wise, discovers that life is a mixture of good days and bad, victory and defeat, give and take.

2. He learns that it doesn't pay to be a sensitive soul; that he should let some things go over his head.

3. He learns that he who loses his temper usually loses out.

4. He learns that all men have burnt toast for breakfast now and then, and that he shouldn't take the other fellow's grouch too seriously.

5. He learns that the quickest way to become unpopular is to carry tales and gossip about others.

6. He learns that "buck-passing" always turns out to be a boomerang.

7. He learns it doesn't matter so much who gets the credit so long as the business prospers.

8. He learns that most other persons are as ambitious as he is, that they have brains as good or better, and that hard work and not cleverness is the secret of success.

9. He learns that no man ever got to first base alone, and it is only through co-operative effort that we move on to better things.

10. He learns that folks are not any harder to get along with in one place than another, and that getting along depends about 98% on his own behavior.

IDEALS

To be myself—

To keep a laugh in heart and throat—

To be good as some friends think I am—

To find joy in my work rather than in the prospect of applause—

To win friends by being one—

To be captain rather than victim of my moods—

To waste neither time nor energy in anticipating calamities which may never come—

To rejoice in the rise of a rival, swift in applauding, and slow in minimizing his success—

To wipe up spilt milk as best I can and hold onto the pan next time—

To be worthy in some measure of the words inscribed on the Chinese Gordon's monument:

"Who at all times and everywhere gave his strength to the weak, his substance to the poor, his sympathy to the suffering, and his heart to God."—*Anon.*

INFORMATION

INFORMATION vs. FACTS

Napoleon Hill says no accurate thinker will pass judgment until he can differentiate between information and facts. Often when someone is being slandered, and another one asks the source of information, one replies: "The paper says, or they say." This is perhaps only information. Upon investigation, the facts may be entirely different, as the following incident proves:

Once a newspaper man, who was unable to get an audience with Edison or get any startling information from his fellow workers, decided to write one himself. The information was that Edison had invented an extraordinary shirt — one that would keep clean for twelve months. He declared that the front of the shirt was made up of 365 very thin layers of a certain fibrous material, the composition being known only to the inventor. Each morning all the wearer had to do, to restore it to its spotlessness, was to tear off one of the layers.

This story was published in five hundred newspapers. Immediately Edison received orders for hundreds of shirts. At first he wrote, informing these buyers that this story was false. But the letters continued to come in such numbers that this became impossible. Many enclosed checks, which had to be returned. The story was published in foreign papers. People from China to Africa all wanted shirts. For more than a year orders kept coming until finally people became aware of the fact that there were no shirts!

JUDGING

JUDGING EACH OTHER

If you must judge us, judge us for what we strive for.

If we are weak, be tolerant.

If we are strong, pray that we become not arrogant.

If our mistakes injure you, tell us of them, and trust in our sense of justice to make reparation.

If we cannot agree on details, such as politics or religion, then let us agree on the broader principle of human kindness; for when we put aside the accumulation of opinions that are the children of self-interest, we will find family resemblance in the faces of men.—*Anon.*

* * * *

We see the world not as it is, but as we are.

The English writer, Charles Lamb, said one day: "I hate that man."

"But you don't know him," a listener objected.

"Of course, I don't," said Lamb. "Do you think I could possibly hate a man I know?"

* * * *

A man's character is revealed best by his speech.—*Proverb.*

* * * *

We should not judge of a man's merit by his good qualities, but by the use he can make of them.—*La Rochefoucauld.*

* * * *

Judge people by moral worth, not by social position.

KINDNESS

BREAD UPON THE WATERS

During a festive celebration in a small town of Pennsylvania, two strangers sought a room in a small hotel.

"We have no room," apologetically answered the manager.

"Neither has any other hotel in own," replied the strangers. "We have been in every one, and there is no room to be found, anywhere."

Sympathetically, the hotel manager said: "You

may have my room. It isn't very fancy, but you take it; I can get along nicely."

The strangers gratefully accepted the offer. Just before checking out the next morning, the benefactor said to the hotel manager: "Some day you'll be the manager of the best and largest of hotels, and perhaps I will build it for you."

The manager smiled but thought nothing more of it.

Several years later, he received an invitation and ticket by mail to come to New York. The manager accepted, mostly out of curiosity. Upon arriving he was met at the train by the man he had once befriended.

"Let's take a little walk," he suggested.

Together they walked down Fifth Avenue and Thirty-Third Street.

"Once I told you that you would be the manager of the best and largest hotel, and that perhaps I would build it for you. Here it is."

There stood one of the world's largest and most exclusive hotels — the Waldorf-Astoria.

Charles Bat became its first manager.

* * * *

Do it this very moment!
Don't put it off — don't wait!
There's no use in doing a kindness
If you do it a day too late!

—*Kingsley.*

KNOWLEDGE

Minds are like parachutes. They function only when they are open.—*Lord Dewar.*

* * * *

That there should one man die ignorant who had capacity for knowledge, this I call a tragedy. —*Thomas Carlyle.*

* * * *

How many a man has dated a new era in his life from the reading of a book?

* * * *

A proverb is a short sentence based on long experience.—*Cervantes.*

* * * *

Only one can keep a secret.—*Anon.*

* * * *

Men are most apt to believe what they least understand.—*Michel de Montaigne.*

* * * *

Iron rusts from disuse; stagnant water loses its purity, and in cold weather becomes frozen; even so does inaction sap the vigor of the mind.— *Da Vinci.*

* * * *

Whoever acquires knowledge but does not practise it, is like one who ploughs a field but does not sow it.

* * * *

On one occasion Aristotle was asked how

much educated men were superior to those uneducated. "As much," said he, "as the living are
to the dead."

Education is an ornament in prosperity and a
refuge in adversity.—*Aristotle.*

LAUGHTER

I have always believed that a good laugh was
good for both the mental and physical digestion.
—*Lincoln.*

* * * *

The most wasted of all days is that on which
we have not laughed.—*S. R. N. Chamfort.*

LOVE

We are shaped and fashioned by what we
love.—*Goethe.*

* * * *

Let me not to the marriage of true minds
Admit impediments. Love is not love
Which alters when it alteration finds,
Or bends with the remover to remove.
Oh, no! It is an ever-fixed mark
That looks on tempests and is never shaken.

It is the star to every wandering bark,
Whose worth's unknown, although his height
    be taken.
Love's not time's fool, though rosy lips and
    cheeks
Within his bending sickle's compass come.
Love alters not with his brief hours and weeks
But bears it out even to the edge of doom.
If this be error and upon me proved,
I never writ, nor no man ever loved.

                          —*Shakespeare.*

*   *   *   *

They do not love that do not show their love.
—*Shakespeare.*

*   *   *   *

Love gives itself; it is not bought.—*Longfellow.*

*   *   *   *

So long as we love we serve; so long as we are
loved by others, I would almost say that we are
indispensable, and no man is useless while he has
a friend.—*Anon.*

*   *   *   *

We pardon to the extent that we love.—*La
Rochefoucauld.*

*   *   *   *

Lovers never get tired of each other because
they are always talking about themselves.—*La
Rochefoucauld.*

If thou wishest to be loved, love—*Seneca.*

* * * *

To be trusted is a greater compliment than to be loved.—*Macdonald.*

MARRIAGE

A person's character is but half formed until after wedlock.—*C. Simmons.*

* * * *

Maids want nothing but husbands, and when they have them, they want everything.—*Shakespeare.*

* * * *

"Long experience has taught me how to figure an appointment with my wife," a businessman once said. "She is always punctually thirty minutes late."

* * * *

Marriage is like a cafeteria. You look the possibilities over carefully, select what you like best, and pay later.

MERCY

The nearer we get to our Heavenly Father, the more we are disposed to look with compassion on perishing souls; we feel that we want to take them upon our shoulders and cast their sins behind our backs. If you would have God have mercy on you, have mercy on one another.—*Joseph Smith.*

MISFORTUNE

If all the misfortunes of mankind were cast into a public stack in order to be equally distributed among the whole species, those who now think themselves the most unhappy would prefer the share they are already possessed of before that which would fall to them by such a division.—*Socrates.*

* * * *

What Cicero said of men — that they are like wines, age souring the bad, and bettering the good — we can say of misfortune, that it has the same effect upon them.—*Richter.*

* * * *

Every billow that comes rolling on to toss us on its crest, is just nature's way to teach us how to do our level best.

If we learn each billow's lesson, 'tis an aid our lives to guide,

If we pass it by unheeded, we're just drifting with the tide.

So when trials and tribulations come to fill your mind with doubt,

They're to teach some needed lesson
You could never learn without.—*Anon.*

* * * *

Everyone can master a grief but he that has it.—*Shakespeare.*

Life is like a grindstone — whether it polishes you up or grinds you down depends on the stuff one is made of.

MISTAKES

Six mistakes of life:

1. The delusion that individual advancement is made by crushing others down.

2. The tendency to worry about a thing that cannot be changed or corrected.

3. Insisting that a thing is impossible because we ourselves have not accomplished it.

4. Refusing to set aside trivial preferences in order that important things may be accomplished.

5. Attempting to compel others to believe and live as we do.

6. The failure to establish the habit of saving money.—*Anon.*

* * * *

All men make mistakes, no matter how big they are. Henry Ford forgot to put a reverse gear

into his first automobile and Edison once spent
two million dollars on an invention which proved
of little value.

* * * *

A teacher sent the following note home with
a six-yearold boy: "He is too stupid to learn."
That boy was Thomas A. Edison!

* * * *

Zaccheus Greeley — the father of Horace —
exclaimed in anger one day: "That boy will never
get along in this world by himself. He'll never
know more than enough to come in out of the
rain."

* * * *

The mother of Benjamin Franklin's wife objected to her daughter marrying Benjamin because
he was a printer. There were already two print-
ing presses in the United States, and she was
afraid the people couldn't support a third one.

* * * *

In the seventeenth century, lawyers were considered of little account, especially penniless ones.
For this reason a Puritan minister serioiusly objected to his daughter marrying one. Despite all
objections. Abigail Smith married her lawyer
friend, John. Thirty years later the husband, John
Adams, became the second President of the
United States.

MISERY

If you wish to be miserable, think about yourself, about what you want, what you like, what respect people ought to pay you, what people think of you; and then to you nothing will be pure. You will spoil everything you touch; you will make sin and misery for yourself out of everything God sends you; you will be as wretched as you choose.—*Charles Kingsley.*

* * * *

It is not the place, nor the condition, but the mind alone that can make anyone happy or miserable.—*L'Estrange.*

* * * *

No one is really miserable who has not tried to cheapen life.—*Anon.*

MUSIC

The man that hath no music in himself,
Nor is not moved with concord of sweet sounds
Is fit for treasons, stratagems, and spoils;
The motions of his spirit are dull as night
And his affections dark as Erebus.
Let no such man be trusted.—*Shakespeare.*

OPPORTUNITY

Once when Henry Ford visited Martha Berry's school in Rome, Georgia, he was asked to contribute a dime to promote school interests.

Martha Berry bought a dime's worth of raw peanuts and planted them. A few years later Mr. Ford made another visit to the school. He was overwhelmed when shown the bank account accrued from the dime's worth of peanuts. Mr. Ford was so delighted that he contributed a building for the school, and later several others.

* * * *

Four things come not back:

> The spoken word,
> The sped arrow,
> The past life,
> The neglected opportunity.

—Arabian Proverb.

* * * *

There is a tide in the affairs of men, which, taken at the flood, leads on to fortune; omitted, all the voyage of their life is bound in shallows and in miseries; and we must take the current when it serves, or lose or ventures.—*Shakespeare.*

OPTIMISM

THE OPTIMISTIC FROG

Two frogs fell in a deep bowl,
One was an optimistic soul,
But the other took the gloomy view.
"We shall drown," he cried without more adieu.
So with a last despairing cry
He flung up his legs and said good-bye.
Quoth the other frog with a merry grin,
"I can't get out, but I won't give in;
I'll just swim around till my strength is spent,
Then will I die the more content."
Bravely he swam till it would seem
His struggles began to churn the cream.
On top of the butter at last he stopped,
And out of the bowl he gaily hopped.
What of the moral? 'Tis easily found:
If you can't hop out, keep swimming around.

—Anon.

PAIN

Pain stayed so long I said to him today,
"I will not have you with me any more";
I stamped my foot and said, "Be on your way,"
And paused there, startled at the look he wore.
"I, who have been your friend," he said to me;

"I, who have been your teacher — all you know
Of understanding love, of sympathy
And patience, I have taught you. Shall I go?"

He spoke the truth, this strange unwelcome guest;
I watched him leave, and knew that he was wise.
He left a heart grown tender in my breast,
He left a far, clear vision in my eyes.
I dried my tears and lifted up a song—
Even for one who'd tortured me so long.

—*Grace Noll Crowell.*

PATIENCE

He that has patience can have what he will.—
Franklin.

PERSEVERANCE

Perseverance is more prevailing than violence;
and many things which cannot be overcome when
they are together yield themselves up when taken
little by little.—*Plutarch.*

* * * *

Time ripens all things. No man is born wise.

* * * *

No one would ever have crossed the ocean if
he could have gotten off the ship in a storm.—
Anon.

For every evil under the sun,
There is a remedy, or there is none.
If there be one, try to find it;
If there be none, never mind it.

❈ ❈ ❈ ❈

The glory is not in never falling, but in rising every time you fall.—*Chinese Proverb.*

PLEASURE

Most pleasures, like flowers, when gathered die.—*Young.*

Avoid popularity; it has many snares, and no real benefit.—*Penn.*

PRAYER

THE PARENT'S PRAYER

O Master, make me a better parent.

Teach me to understand my children, to listen patiently to what they have to say, and to answer all the questions kindly. Keep me from interrupting them, talking back to them, and contradicting them. Make me as courteous to them as I would have them be to me. Give me the courage to confess my sins against my children and to ask their forgiveness, when I know that I have done them a wrong.

May I not vainly hurt the feelings of my children. Forbid that I should laugh at their mistakes or resort to shame and ridicule as punishment. Let me not tempt my child to lie and to steal. So guide me hour by hour that I may demonstrate by all I say and do that honesty produces happiness.

Reduce, I pray, the meanness in me. May I cease to nag; and when I am out of sorts, help me to hold my tongue.

Blind me to the little errors of my children and help me see the good things that they do. Give me a ready word for honest praise.

Help me to grow up with my children, to treat them as I would those of their own age; but let me not exact of them the judgment and conventions of adults. Allow me not to rob them of the opportunity to wait upon themselves, to think, to choose, and to make decisions.

Forbid that I should ever punish them for my selfish satisfaction. May I grant them all their wishes that are reasonable and have the courage always to withhold a privilege which I know will do them harm.

Make me so fair and just, so considerate and companionable to my children that they will have a genuine esteem for me. Fit me to be loved and imitated.

With all thy gifts, O great Master, give me calm, poise, and self-control.—*Author Unknown*.

* * * *

He asked for strength that he might achieve,
He was made weak that he might obey.
He asked for health that he might do greater things.
He was given infirmity that he might do better things.
He asked for riches that he might be happy,
He was given poverty that he might be wise.
He asked for power that he might have the praise of men,
He was given weakness that he might feel the need of God.
He asked for all things that he might enjoy life,
He was given life that he might enjoy all things.
He has received nothing that he asked for,
All that he hoped for,
His prayer is answered; he is most blessed.

—*Anon.*

* * * *

Until we have prayed, we cannot do more than pray. After we have prayed, we can do more.

If you cannot pray over a thing and cannot ask God to bless you in it, don't do that thing. A secret that you would keep from God is a secret that you should keep from your own heart.— *Tholuch.*

✤ ✤ ✤ ✤

What men usually ask for when they pray to God is that two and two may not make four.— *Russian Proverb.*

✤ ✤ ✤ ✤

Work as if everything depended upon you, and pray as if everything depended upon God.— *Anon.*

PRESCIENCE

TEACHING A MACHINE TO SAY "SPEZIA"

The discovery of the principle of the phonograph has been described by Mr. Edison:

"I was singing to the mouthpiece of a telephone, when the vibrations of the voice sent the fine steel point into my finger. That set me to thinking. If I could record the actions of the point, and send the point over the same surface afterward, I saw no reason why the thing would not talk.

"I tried the experiment first on a slip of telegraph paper, and found that the point made an alphabet. I shouted the words, 'Halloo! Halloo!' in return.

"I determined to make a machine that would work accurately, and gave my assistants instructions, telling them what I had discovered. They laughed at me. That's the whole story. The phonograph is the result of the pricking of a finger."

No, it was the result of Mr. Edison's pricking his finger. No other man would have persisted as he did in making a machine talk. It took an incredible amount of patient experimenting to make the machine say "I" or "s". His biographer reports that Edison spent fifteen hours a day, or more, for six or seven months, upon such words as "spezia."

"Spezia," roared the inventor.

"Pezia," lisped the phonograph.

And it took thousands of repetitions and manipulations of the machine before the desired result was obtained. The education of the phonograph was a difficult task. A man of the highest scientific attainments would sit for hours, day after day, gravely saying to the machine:

"Mary had a little lamb,
A little lamb, lamb, lamb."

With less perseverance and determination to perfect his work, the machine would have been good for nothing.

* * * *

One day a little frog fell in a large rut that a

wagon wheel had made. He tried and tried to get out, but was unsuccessful.

A frog friend heard of his plight and came to see if he could help. To his amazement he found that his friend had managed to get out.

"How did you finally do it?"

"I had to," replied the frog. "A wagon was coming."

❦ ❦ ❦ ❦

Great souls suffer in silence—*Schiller*.

❦ ❦ ❦ ❦

The gem cannot be polished without friction, nor man perfected without trials.—*Chinese proverb*.

❦ ❦ ❦ ❦

STEP BY STEP

If but one message I may leave behind,
One single word of courage for my kind,
It would be this—Oh, brother, sister, friend,
Whatever life may bring, what God may send,
No matter whether clouds lift soon or late,
Take heart and wait.

Despair may tangle darkly at your feet,
Your faith be dimmed, and hope, once cool and
    sweet,
Be lost; but suddenly above a hill,
A heavenly lamp, set on a heavenly sill

Will shine for you and point the way to go.
How well I know.

Repeatedly—it has not failed me yet.
For I have waited through the dark, and I
Have seen a star rise in the blackest sky
Repeatedly it has not failed one yet.

And I have learned God never will forget
To light His lamp. If we but wait for it,
It will be lit.—*Grace Noll Crowell.*

REPENTANCE

Of all the acts of man repentance is the most divine.—*Carlyle.*

*   *   *   *

Some often repent, yet never reform; they resemble a man traveling in a dangerous path, who frequently starts and stops, but never turns back.—*Thornton.*

*   *   *   *

There are two kinds of repentance: One is that of Judas, the other that of Peter; the one is ice broken, the other ice melted. Repentance unto life will be repentance in the life.—*William Nevins.*

*   *   *   *

A grindstone that had not grit in it, how long

would it take to sharpen an axe? And affairs that had not grit in them, how long would they take to make a man?—*Beecher.*

REPUTATION

Reputation is seeming; character is being.

Reputation is manufactured; character is grown.

Reputation is your photograph; character is your face.

Reputation is what men say you are; character is what God knows you are.

Reputation is what you need to get a job; character is what you need to keep it.

Reputation is what comes over you from without; character is what rises up within.

Reputation is what you have when you come to town; character is what you have when you go away.

Reputation is what is chiseled on your tombstone; character is what the angels say about you before the throne of God.—*Anon.*

* * * *

To be great is to be misunderstood.—*Emerson.*

REVENGE

Revenge is a common passion; it is the sin of the uninstructed. The savage deems it noble; but the religion of Christ, which is the sublime civilizer, emphatically condemns it. Why? Because religion ever seeks to ennoble man; and nothing so debases him as revenge.—*Bulwer Lytton.*

* * * *

By taking revenge, a man is but even with his enemy; but in passing over it, he is superior.— *Bacon.*

* * * *

Revenge is like a boomerang. Although for a time it flies in the direction in which it is hurled, it takes a sudden curve, and returning hits your own head the heaviest blow of all.— Anon.

* * * *

To revenge is no valor, but to bear.—*Shakespeare.*

SELF-IMPROVEMENT

By all means sometimes be alone; salute thyself; see what thy soul doth wear; dare to look in thy chest, and tumble up and down what thou findest there.—*Wordsworth.*

✦ ✦ ✦ ✦

You will find that the mere resolve not to be useless, and the honest desire to help other people, will, in the quickest and delicatest ways, improve yourself.—*Ruskin.*

✦ ✦ ✦ ✦

People seldom improve when they have no other model but themselves to copy after.—*Goldsmith.*

SCARS

Life wounds all of us. At best there is sorrow enough to go round. Yet because the deepest wounds are those of the soul and hidden to mortal sight, we keep hurting each other day by day, inflicting wounds that time mercifully scars over. But the scars remain, ready at a touch to throb angrily and ache again with the old gnawing wild pain.

You remember that day in school when the

teacher laughed? You were only a little fellow, shy and silent, sitting in the shadow of the big boys, wistfully looking toward the day when you would shine as they did.

That day you were sure your chance had come. You were sure that you had just what the teacher wanted on the tip of your tongue, and you jumped up and shouted it out loudly and eagerly, triumphantly—and you were very, very wrong.

There followed a flash of astonishment, an instant of dreadful silence, and then the room rang with mirth. You heard only the teacher's laughter, and it drowned your heart.

Many years have gone over your head since that day, but the sight of a little lad trudging along to school brings it back, and the old pain stirs and beats against the scar. You cover it over, hush it to quiet once more with a smile. "I must have been funny. She couldn't help it." But you wish she had.

And there was that time when your best friend failed you. When the loose-tongued gossips started the damaging story and he was pressed for a single word in your defense, he said, "Oh, he's all right. Of course, he's all right, but I don't want to get mixed up in this thing. Can't afford it. Have to think of my own name and my own family, you understand. Good fellow, but I have to keep out of this."

You felt forsaken. For weeks and weeks you carried the pain in your heart. The story was bad enough but would right itself. The idea that he should fail you, that he had not rushed to your side at the first hint of trouble was bad enough, was unbearable. He came back again after it was all over, but the sight of him renewed the ache in your breast and the throb of pain in your throat. The scar was thin, and the hurt soul beneath it quivered.

We all bear scars. Life is a struggle, and hurts must come. But why the unnecessary ones? Why hurt the souls of little children? Why say things to them that they must remember with pain all their lives? Why say the smart, tart thing that goes straight to the heart of someone we love because we would relieve ourselves of the day's tension and throw off a grain of the soul's bitterness?

Who are we to inflict wounds and suffering and scars on those about us? Staggering, blind mortals, groping our way from somewhere "here" to somewhere "there" conscious of little but the effort to stay "here" a little longer!

It behooves us to travel softly, regardful of one another's happiness, particularly where our path crosses that of those dependent upon us for comfort or enters into the heart of little children.—*Author unknown.*

SIN

Seven deadly sins:
> Knowledge without character.
> Business without morality.
> Science without humanity.
> Worship without sacrifice.
> Pleasure without conscience.
> Politics without principle.
> Wealth without works. —*Anon.*

SLANDER

If anyone tells you a person speaks ill of you, do not make excuse about what is said but answer, "He was ignorant of my other faults else he would not have mentioned these alone."—*Epictetus.*

* * * *

No soul of high estate can take pleasure in slander. It betrays a weakness.—*Pascal.*

* * * *

He that cannot forgive others breaks the bridge over which he himself must pass if he would ever reach heaven, for everyone has need to be forgiven.—*Herbert.*

When a bee stings, she dies. She cannot sting and live. When men sting, their better selves die. Every sting kills a better instinct. Men must not turn bees and kill themselves in stinging others.—*Bacon.*

If I were to try to read, much less answer, all the attacks made on me, this shop might as well be closed for other business. I do the very best I know — the very best I can — and I mean to keep doing so until the end. If the end brings me out all right, what is said against me won't amount to anything. If the end brings me out wrong, ten angels swearing I was right would make no difference.—*Abraham Lincoln.*

* * * *

A story that has to be told in an undertone might just as well be left unsaid.

SMILES

VALUE OF SMILES

Smile on folk, and you will find that they will
    smile on you —
Really it's surprising what a little smile can do.
Wear one with your working clothes and with
    your Sunday best.
Wear a cheery smile, and you will always feel
    well dressed.

Doesn't really matter about quality and style,
Even shabby things don't look so bad, worn
    with a smile.
Give a smile and take a smile, and say a word
    of cheer.
A smile won't grow old-fashioned like the hat
    you wore last year.
A smile suits any kind of face: a smile is always
    smart.
For smiles reveal the sunshine that is shining in
    your heart.   *—Author Unknown.*

The most recent definition of a philosopher:
one who instead of crying over spilt milk con-
soles himself with the thought that it was over
four-fifths water.—*Anon.*

To miss the chance of service,
To fail to speak the word of kindness,
Not to impart something of our strength
And goodwill to those who need them—
This is the sin that finds little chance of
    atonement.   *—Anon.*

*   *   *   *

The greatest fault, I should say, is to be conscious of none.—*Carlyle.*

*   *   *   *

The worst effect of sin is wtihin and is mani-
fest not in poverty, and pain, and bodily deface-
ment, but in the discrowned faculties, the un-

worthy love, the low ideal, the brutalized and en-
slaved spirit.—*E. H. Chapin.*

* * * *

As sins proceed, they ever multiply; and like
figures in arithmetic, the last stands for more
than all that went before it.—*Browne.*

* * * *

Bad men hate sin through fear of punishment; good men hate sin through their love of
virtue.—*Juvenal.*

* * * *

There is no sin we can be tempted to commit,
but we shall find a greater satisfaction in resist-
ing than in committing.

* * * *

We are saved from nothing if we are not saved
from sin. Little sins are pioneers of hell.—*Howell.*

It is not only what we do, but also what we
do not do, for which we are accountable.—*Mo-
liere.*

* * * *

Sins are like circles in the water when a stone
is thrown into it; one produces another. When
anger was in Cain's heart, murder was not far
off.—*Philip Henry.*

* * * *

If I grapple with sin in my own strength, the
devil knows he may go to sleep.—*H. G. J. Adams.*

It is not true that there are no enjoyments in the ways of sin; there are, many and various. But the great and radical defect of them all is that they are transitory and unsubstantial, at war with reason and conscience, and always leave a sting behind. We are hungry, and they offer us bread; but it is poisoned bread. We are thirsty, and they offer us drink; but it is from deadly fountains. They may and often do satisfy us for the moment, but it is death in the end. It is only the bread of heaven and the water of life that can so satisfy that we shall hunger no more and thirst no more forever.—*Tyron Edwards.*

SORROW

The deeper the sorrow the less tongue it hath.— *Talmud.*

* * * *

There are no crown-wearers in heaven that were not cross-bearers here below—*Spurgeon.*

* * * *

Behind the clouds is the sun still shining;
Be still, sad heart! and cease repining,
Thy fate is the common fate of all;
Into each life some rain must fall;
Some days must be dark, and dreary—*Long-fellow.*

There is no flock, however watched and tended,
But one dead lamb is there!
There is no fireside, howsoever defended
But has one vacant chair—*Longfellow*.

* * * *

If none were sick and none were sad,
What service could we render?
I think if we were always glad,
We scarcely could be tender.
Did our beloved never need
Our patient ministration,
Earth would grow cold and miss indeed
Its sweet consolation.
If sorrow never claimed our heart,
And every wish were granted,
Patience would die, and hope depart.
Life would be disenchanted—*Anon*.

* * * *

There are lots of other folks you can be
sorry for stead of yourself— *From the book Chins
Up*.

* * * *

Everyone can master a grief, but he that has
it—*Shakespeare*.

* * * *

When I am attacked by gloomy thoughts,
nothing helps me so much as running to my
books; they quickly absorb me and banish the
clouds from my mind—*Montaigne*.

Sorrow is a fruit: God does not make it grow on limbs too weak to bear it—*Victor Hugo*.

* * * *

The most disastrous times have produced the greatest minds. The purest metal comes of the most ardent furnace, the most brilliant lightning comes from the darkest clouds—*Chateaubriand*.

WHAT KILLED THE EAGLE

Some shepherds once saw an eagle soar out from a crag. It flew majestically far up into the sky, but by and by became unsteady and began to waver in its flight. At length one wing dropped, and then the other, and the poor bird fell swiftly to the ground. The shepherds sought the fallen bird and found that a little serpent had fastened itself upon it while resting on the crag. The eagle did not know that the serpent was there. But it crawled in through the feathers; and, while the proud monarch was sweeping through the air, the serpent's fangs were thrust into his flesh, and he came reeling into the dust.

It is the story of many a life. Some secret sin has long been eating its way into the heart, and at last the proud life lies soiled and dishonored in the dust.

Happy indeed is the youth who learns to hate all impurity of imagination or indelicacy of thought, or speech, or conduct. Lord Tennyson, to whom we are indebted for so many beautiful words, makes Sir Galahad, one of his noblest heroes, say—

> My strength is as the strength of ten,
> Because my heart is pure.

TOMORROW

A bright little boy with laughing face,
Whose every motion was full of grace,
Who knew no trouble and feared no care,
Was the light of our household, the youngest
    there.

He was too young, this little elf,
With troublesome questions to vex himself;
But for many days a thought would arise,
And bring a shade to the dancing eyes.

He went to one whom he thought more wise
Than any other beneath the skies;
"Mother"—oh, word that makes the home!—
"Tell me when will tomorrow come?"

"It is almost night," the mother said,
"And time for my boy to be in bed;
When you wake up, it's day again;
It will be tomorrow, my darling, then."

The little boy slept through all the night
But woke with the first red streaks of light;
He pressed a kiss on his mother's brow,
And whispered, "Is it tomorrow now?"

"No, little Eddie, this is today;
Tomorrow is always one night away."
He pondered awhile, but joys came fast,
And the vexing question quickly passed.

But it came again with the shades of night;
"Will it be tomorrow when it is light?"
From years to come he seemed care to borrow;
He tried so hard to catch tomorrow.

"You cannot catch it, my little Ted;
Enjoy today," the mother said:
"Some wait for tomorrow through many a year—
It always is coming, but never is here."—*Anonymous.*

* * * *

Finish every day and be done with it. You have done what you could; some blunders and absurdities crept in; forget them as soon as you can. Tomorrow is a new day; you shall begin it well and serenely and with too high a spirit to be encumbered with your old nonsense.—*Emerson.*

* * * *

Our grand business is not to see what lies

dimly in the distance, but to do what lies clearly
at hand.—*Carlyle.*

When people yearn with all their hearts
For just one treasure far away;
They close their eyes to countless joys
That crowd around them every day.—
Anon.

* * * *

Eternity is an endless chain of nows.

* * * *

One minute of *do it now,* is of more value
than ages of *put it off.*—*Anon.*

* * * *

By the street of by and by, one arrives at
the house of never.—*Cervantes.*

* * * *

Lose this day by loitering—it will be the
same story tomorrow, and the next more dila-
tory.

VICE

What maintains one vice would bring up
two children.—*Benjamin Franklin.*

VIRTUE

To be able under all circumstances to practise five things constitutes perfect virtue; these five are gravity, generosity of soul, sincerity, earnestness, and kindness.—*Confucius.*

* * * *

We rarely like the virtues we have not.—*Shakespeare.*

* * * *

It has been my experience that folks who have no vices have very few virtues.—*Lincoln.*

* * * *

We need greater virtues to sustain good fortune than bad.—*La Rochefoucauld.*

* * * *

A thankful heart is not only the greatest virtue, but also the parent of all other virtues.—*Cicero.*

* * * *

He that plants thorns must never expect to gather roses.—*Pilpay.*

* * * *

Sometime we may learn more from a man's errors than from his virtues.—*Franklin.*

* * * *

Never rise to speak until you have something to say, and when you have said it cease.

If I can only keep my good name, I shall have riches enough.—*Plautus.*

* * * *

The surest proof of being endowed with noble qualities is to be free from envy.—*La Rochefoucauld.*

WORK

In order that people may be happy in their work these three things are needed: They must be fit for it. They must not do too much of it. And they must have a sense of success in it.—*Ruskin.*

* * * *

If people knew how hard I have had to work to gain my mastery, it wouldn't seem wonderful at all.—*Michelangelo.*

* * * *

I shall never ask, never refuse, nor ever resign an office.—*Franklin.*

* * * *

Little strokes fell great oaks.—*Franklin.*

* * * *

He that riseth late must trot all day.—*Franklin.*

Many lives fail from inability to deliver the last blow; a workman lifts his iron maul repeatedly upon the plow until the deed is done. Which blow split the rock? They all did, but without the last one the first one and all between would have come to nothing.

* * * *

He is not only idle who does nothing, but he is idle who might be better employed.—*Socrates.*

* * * *

The man who removed the mountain began by carrying away small stones.—*Chinese Proverb.*

** * * *

It is better to wear out than rust out.—*Cumberland.*

WORTH

THE GREATEST WORK

He built a house; time laid it in the dust;
He wrote a book, its title now forgot.
He ruled a city, but his name is not
On any table graven, or where rust
Can gather from disuse, or marble bust.
He took a child from out a wretched cot
Who on the state dishonor might have brought
And reared him to the Christian's hope and trust,

The boy to manhood grown, became a light
To many souls, and preached for human need
The wondrous love of the Omnipotent.
The work has multiplied like stars at night
When darkness deepens; every noble deed
Lasts longer than a granite monument.—*Author
Unknown*.

VALUES UNKNOWN

Nobody knows what a boy is worth,
A boy with his face aglow,
For hid in his heart there are secrets deep,
Not even the wisest know.
Nobody knows what a boy is worth,
A boy with his bare, white feet,
So have a smile and kindly word,
For every boy you meet.
Nobody knows what a boy is worth,
A boy at his work or play,
A boy who whistles around the place
Or laughs in an artless way.
Nobody knows what a boy is worth,
And the world must wait to see,
For every man in an honored place
Is a boy that used to be.—*Anon*.